○Tools for life

LifeShapes for youth

○Rich Atkinson

Tools for life: Lifeshapes for youth
Rich Atkinson and the Rebuild team

©Copyright 2014 Rich Atkinson

For information write to:
REBUILD
147A Upperthorpe Road
Sheffield, S6 3EB, UK

First Published 2014
Published by 3DM Publishing

ISBN 978-0-9907775-8-8

3DM Publishing

A few thanks

A big thanks to Amanda Curtis and my wife, Lizzie, who spent hours editing my messy original manuscript and turned it into something that makes sense. I'm so grateful to you both.

Secondly, I'm so thankful for the people I get to journey with on the Rebuild team. You are passionate followers of Jesus who spur me on to be all I can be and encourage me to use the LifeShape tools effectively in my life.

Contents

Introduction

Getting started

'Listen to these three key instructions' was the last thing I heard as I disengaged my brain and began to chat to one of my friends. I was 15 and, as a youth group, we were going horse riding for the first time as an activity on a weekend away. I had complained that morning about doing such a dull activity and was busy telling my friend how stupid it was that they had an 'instructor' for something as simple as riding a horse!

'You just sit on the thing', I complained to my mate as the instructor droned on.

I discovered later that the instructor had told everyone that there were three key things that you should never do when riding a horse. These were: don't drop the reins; don't let your feet fall out of the stirrups; and, whatever you do, don't panic!

Eventually it was time to set off on our horses. I stopped

chatting to my friend as the instructor turned his horse and set off. One by one each of the horses trotted off in pursuit of the lead horse, including mine.

Unfortunately, the bumping of the horse beneath me led me to immediately drop the reins, my feet fell out of the stirrups and I totally panicked! I clung to the hair on the mane of the poor horse and pleadingly screamed for it to stop. The screaming seemed to provoke the horse to sense that it should help get its rider out of trouble by running faster! By the time the instructor had managed to stop the horse, calm it down and give me a telling off for not listening, my knuckles were white from clinging on so tightly and my pride had taken a rather significant dent.

Many of the young people I know have experiences in their walk with God that are rather like my horse riding experience. I often have this problem as I hare off in my spiritual life without the necessary tools in place and then wonder why it didn't always work out as well as I'd hoped.

In my experience, there is nothing more exciting than young people filled with passion for Jesus *and* equipped with the right tools. After all, the young disciples that Jesus picked up were full of passion. He spent three years giving them tools to live out that passion and then they changed the world. We want to be people that change the world with the fire that's in our bellies and the right tools in our hands. Young people are the best bringers of change in society and when they're fired up, living lives equipped with the right tools, they ALWAYS see amazing things happen!

This book is for young people who want the chance to engage with some simple tools that will enable them to run fast without falling off!

Let's get this adventure started...

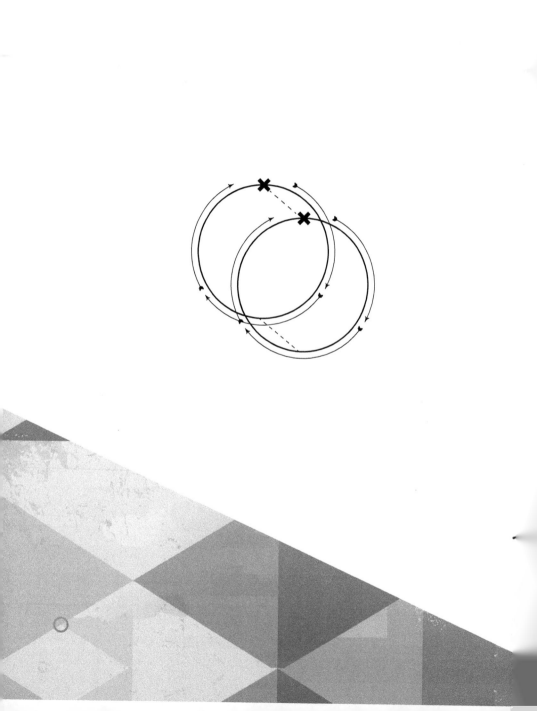

1

Learning to learn

the Circle

Have you ever watched the early rounds of X-Factor, American Idol, Britain's Got Talent or a similar show? I don't know about you but I often wonder why people with clearly no musical talent whatsoever put themselves in front of the world to display their lack of ability to sing. Simon Cowell sits behind his desk and hits them with one of his famous lines. One amazing Cowell put down was on an American Idol show when he was listening to a young lady called Jay.

> **Simon:** I've got to stop this. It is so way off WAY off Mariah Carey. It wasn't why I was laughing but...
>
> **Jay:** My voice is strong. I need help.
>
> **Simon:** You do, you need a helpline.

These poor people have this crushing moment where they realise that Simon doesn't think they can sing as well as they thought they could. The people that really amaze and confuse me are the ones that go back year after year ... 'well Simon this is my ninth attempt to prove to you that I can sing', only to be crushed yet again! The question is: why on earth don't these people learn? They can't sing and they need to find something else to have a go at.

Whilst it's amusing to watch these wonderful crash and burn moments I sometimes wonder if God feels the same about us at times ... 'Why on earth don't these people learn?'

This first shape is all about how we learn from the experiences we have so that God can mould and shape us like clay in a potter's hands.

When Jesus was on earth He had a strikingly simple message:

> 'The time has come,' he said. 'The Kingdom of God is near. Repent and believe the good news!'

> Mark 1:15

Jesus basically says to people ... right ... God is near and you can meet Him and get into the kingdom ... Good News ... Only problem is that you have to do something about it.

Jesus says that there are two parts to this:

Repent

We get a bit mixed up with the word repent when we read it in the Bible because we often think of it as meaning the same as apologise. The people hearing Jesus would have understood it quite differently. The English word we have in our Bible *repent* is translated from the Greek word *metanoia* which is the original language which the book of Mark was written in.

The Greek word *metanoia* is two words stuck together, the word *meta* which means change and the word *noia* which means thinking. It therefore means **change your thinking**.

With this understanding of the word repent we can see that our American Idol contestant, who has repeatedly been told by Simon that they can't sing, needs to repent! They need to change their thinking about their ability to sing.

Believe

Jesus isn't just interested in what's going on in the mind though. Jesus says that we need to repent (change our thinking) *and* believe.

The Greek word which we read as 'believe' in this verse in Mark is *pisteuo*, which means

> *'to have faith in or upon, a person or thing.'*

When a sports person is being interviewed by a commentator they often say something along the lines of, 'I just believed I could do it'. This belief meant they performed in such a way that they went for every shot because they were putting faith in themselves to win.

The 'believe' that Jesus is talking about here is just as active. It's a case of not just changing your mind but stepping out and living this changed mind in a way that shows that you believe it.

It would be no good if our American Idol contestant changed their thinking about their singing ability but continued with their previous pattern of life, showing up to sing every year for Simon Cowell. They would need to go home, cancel the singing lessons and find something else to put their time, effort and money into!

The Circle Tool

The first tool which we're going to look at is one that helps us learn from events or experiences in our lives in a way that changes our minds and actions to be more like Jesus. We are going to learn how to repent and believe!

> *24 Do you not know that in a race all the runners run, but only one gets the prize? Run in such a way as to get the prize. 25 Everyone who competes in the games goes into strict training. They do it to get a crown that will not last; but we do it to get a crown that will last forever. 26 Therefore I do not run like a man running aimlessly; I do not fight like a man beating the air.*
>
> *1 Corinthians 9:24-26*

Our journey with God is like a race: runners who want to run fast have to learn from their previous races, training sessions, the coaches instructions, and new scientific breakthroughs they discover. We can learn from all sorts of things that can help us grow in our walk with God. Whenever you read the Bible, pray, chat to your friends, listen to talks, do something wrong, do something right, or have experiences in life, you have the chance to grow. Simply hearing the information or having the experience won't necessarily mean you'll learn and grow unless you fully change your thinking and act upon it... **repent and believe**.

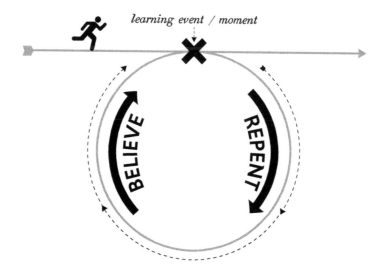

learning event / moment

The diagram above shows this process in action. The line is your life and you can see the runner jogging along. The cross is where one of these possible learning events or moments occurs and gives you the chance to learn from it. You do this by working around the circle to **change your thinking (repent)** and **act upon your changed thinking (believe)**.

Learn from it!

So the question is ... How do we make sure we change our mind and act upon it when these moments occur? We're going to break down the process of repent (changing your mind) and believe (acting upon it) into 6 key stages that you can easily work through anytime you have one of these potential learning events or moments.

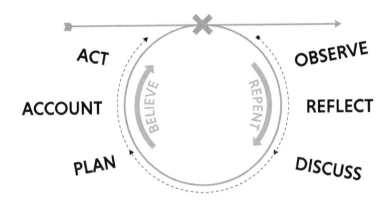

So let's take a few minutes to go through each of these stages. I'll take you through examples from my life where I used these stages to learn effectively from an event.

1. OBSERVE

2. REFLECT

3. DISCUSS

4. PLAN

5. ACCOUNT

6. ACT

Observe

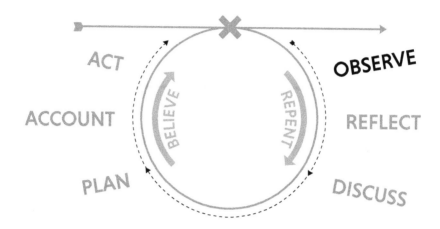

This is the first step of the journey and probably the easiest. It's simply a case of observing what's happened. Usually it's best to do this first step by writing it down.

Write down:

- » What happened?
- » What did you read?
- » What did you do wrong?
- » What did you do right?
- » What did you hear?
- » What did you realise?
- » What did you notice?

Try to write down everything that happened, keep it simple, and just the facts. For example, you may have heard a challenging sermon and so you'd write down what the key points were that struck you and challenged you or made you think. Do it as quickly as possible after the event or moment so that you don't forget key things that happened.

Example

When I was a teenager my friends and I would go to Soul Survivor, a great Christian youth festival in the south of England, and have a fantastic time with God. When I was there I heard a talk about how we need to live a radical life for Jesus all the time and not just every summer at a great festival. I was challenged because I realised that at Soul Survivor I was the most passionate worshipper in the building, but at school some of my friends had no idea about what I believed. I realised that I was living two very different lives and I was challenged that it wasn't right!

My observations:

1. God didn't want me to have two separate lives.
2. I wasn't living the way I wanted to be living around my friends at school.
3. I felt closer to God at the summer festival.

Reflect

There's one key word which you need to remember for the 'reflect' part of the circle and that is:

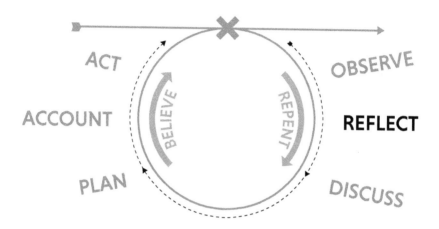

WHY?

You need to sit down and look at what you've observed and ask yourself why? You may want to consider:

> » Why did it happen?
> » Why did I do that?
> » Why did that challenge me?
> » Why did that verse stand out?
> » Why did God say that to me?
> » Why did I react like that?
> » Why did I feel that way?

This is your chance to try and get under the skin of what happened or what challenged you. It's a really key part of the learning process, so take some time over this to try and really understand it.

Example

My reflections:

1. I was fearful of living out my Christian life at school because people might think I was weird and I didn't want to lose any friends.
2. I didn't know how to share my faith with my friends.
3. I hadn't developed my own devotional times well enough so was relying on others to help me connect with God.

Discuss

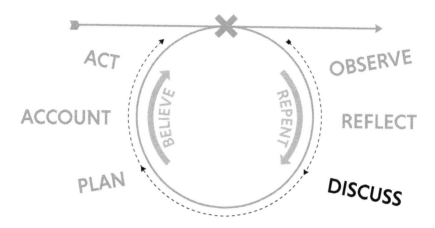

This is the part where you discuss your observation and reflection with someone else. You may want to take it to your small group, your youth leader or a good friend. The reason you do this is because it gives someone the chance to help you by giving you an alternative view.

First, share with them what you have observed and your reflections on that observation. Then ask them to share with you what their reflections are on your learning moment.

1. Why do they think it's a challenge for you?
2. What do they see that you've missed?

This part of learning is vital because sometimes we can't see the situation as clearly as someone else can. Often they'll have observations and reflections that will really help us before we move onto the next step. It's all part of the way God designed us as people that hear God best when we are part of community together with others. None of us are designed to try and do it all on our own.

Example

I discussed my Soul Survivor observation and reflection with two of my friends, who I was surprised and relieved to hear had in fact had very similar experiences. They helped me see that in addition to my reflections they thought that sometimes I could be overly worried about what people thought of me and therefore I'd not be comfortable in trusting in the way that God saw me. They helped me realise that I was insecure in my identity in God. What could have just been another nice sermon was turning out to be a great opportunity to learn and see lots of change in my life.

Plan

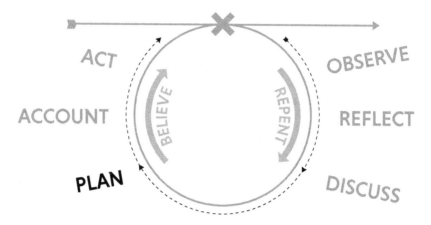

If we're going to do more than just change our mind about something it's important that we make a really good plan about how we are going to do it. To make a really good plan for what you're going to do we recommend you make it a **T.A.R.G.E.T.** plan.

Testing: Make it something that will push you so that you'll be sure to move forward.

Achievable: Make it something that you can actually do. Don't make it so hard you'll never achieve it.

Real: Make a really specific plan. What are the real steps that you will actually take?

God given: Make it something that fits with the God given challenge you received. Does this plan fit with your observations and reflections?

Enabling: Make it something that you do yourself, not something that someone else should do!

Time specific: Make it with a timeframe so you'll know when it will be completed.

Example

My plan was:

1. To buy some bible reading notes and read them every day.
2. To start a prayer group at school with some other Christians I knew to make my worlds collide a little more.
3. To tell one of my friends, within 2 weeks, about my faith.

Account

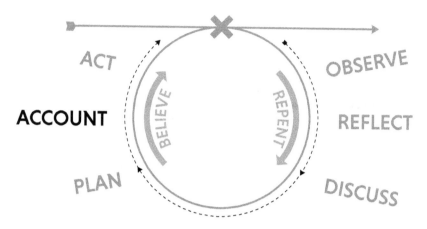

It's very easy to make a plan but it can be a whole lot more difficult to actually follow through with it. The best way to make sure you actually do it is to get someone to hold you to account. This means telling someone else about your plans so that they will keep asking you how you are getting on. It means you have a much better chance of actually doing them!

Give your plan to a friend or your small group. It needs to be people that you'll see regularly. They will need to remember to ask you how you're getting on and be prepared to challenge you if you're not doing what you said you would do.
Firstly, get them to help you see if your plan fits with all the T.A.R.G.E.T. plan pointers and get them to ask you questions about the plan. If nothing needs to change then set a time when you'll next talk about how you're getting on with putting it into action.

Example

I asked my friends, who I had discussed my situation with, to hold me to account. Helpfully, they had made similar plans so we met up every week to discuss how we were doing, pray for one another and challenge each other.

Act

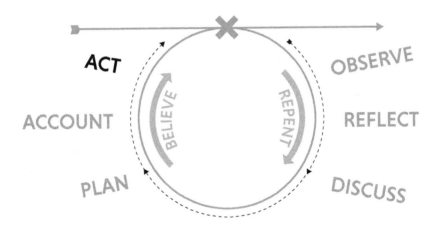

Now it's time to get on and actually do it. This way you'll complete the process of repent and believe. So far all the learning that you've done has been in your head. Your mind has been changed by the observe, reflect and discuss part of the circle. Now you need to see that change of mind turn into real change in your life. We've done the plan and account part of the learning circle, but as James put it in the bible:

Faith without deeds is useless.

James 2:20

Time to get on with it!

Example

I bought some bible reading notes and began to read my bible and pray every day which helped me meet with God and be close to Him no matter what events I had been to recently.

I told one of my friends about God and was surprised about how open and interested he was in what I believed in. I ended up having some amazing conversations with all of my friends who quickly heard about it.

I started a prayer group where we gathered one lunchtime to pray. To my surprise, by the end of the year a couple of my non-Christian friends had actually come along a few times to check it out!

THINK

What's the learning moment that God is challenging you with or speaking to you about?

Who will you process your observations and reflections with?

Who will you ask to hold you accountable for doing your plan?

2

Plugging in

the Semi-Circle

'No it is you ... honest', I said to my younger sister as we played on the games console together. However, the truth was ... it wasn't! I was playing on a single player game when she had come and tried to join in. To my shame I'd got out an old controller and told her that she was the character controlled by the computer and we had sat there playing happily for several minutes without her actually doing anything ... smugly I thought I'd found the perfect solution.

Everyone was a winner. Or so I thought. As the battle continued on the screen in front of us I started to beat the computer character and my sister began to get upset.

'Give me a chance', she said, 'come on I'm younger than you.'

But of course I couldn't give her a chance ... she wasn't actually plugged in.

I performed the last killer move and finally I had the victory. I had defeated the monster and I was onto the next level! The only problem was that my sister burst into tears because she thought I'd beaten her and not given her a chance. My mum dashed in and told me off for not giving my sister enough of an opportunity to win and I had to make the awful confession that I hadn't actually let her play in the first place.

I was in the dog house for some time!

The truth is, we all want to play. We all want to be in the game. We all want to be plugged in. Sometimes though it just seems like we're on a treadmill doing the same old things over and over and over. School, homework, time with friends, bed ... over and over and over.

So how do we plug in?

What do we plug in to? What on earth does it all look like? It says in the bible that Jesus came to give us 'life to the full' (John 10:10)

Again, the question is ... what does this life to the full look like?

Jesus explained how we get plugged into this 'life to the full' in another bit of the bible.

> *I am the vine; you are the branches. If you remain in me and I in you, you will bear much fruit; apart from me you can do nothing.*

> *John 15:5*

Jesus seems to suggest here that we can constantly be plugged into Him. We can be plugged in all the time! The problem is that life has a funny way of being crazy busy at some points, really quiet at others, hard at times, fun at others, exciting at some moments and boring at others. And so the question is, what does this connection with Jesus look like?

I don't know about you, but at times connection to Jesus can feel a little like it did for my little sister on the computer game. It can feel like we're trying so hard to connect and yet we don't seem to really be in control. Between school, homework, working out friendships and playing for the local team it feels like we're clicking on the controller of our lives but everything is just going on around us without much time to stop and connect with Jesus. How on earth do we add time with Jesus into all that? Time to stop, reflect, read the bible, pray and listen to what He is saying to us? I mean *that's* what connection is right?

So should we all just quit it all and become silent nuns?

Thankfully, I don't think that's what Jesus means by being constantly connected to the vine. Let's look again at what He says to us in John 15.

> *"I am the true vine, and my Father is the gardener.* ²
> *He cuts off every branch in me that bears no fruit, while every branch that does bear fruit he prunes so that it will be even more fruitful.* ³ *ou are already clean because of the word I have spoken to you.* ⁴*Remain in me, as I also remain in you. No branch can bear fruit by itself; it must remain in the vine. Neither can you bear fruit unless you remain in me.*

> *John 15:1-4*

So, let's make sure we're together in following this one:

The vine is Jesus

The reason Jesus talks about a vine is because a vine is the central part of a plant which grows grapes. The vine part of the plant which produces a grape acts like the trunk of a tree. It is the central strongest part of the plant and it draws all of the water and nutrients out of the soil and sends it to branches so that they can produce grapes.

The yummy exciting bit that makes grape juice and wine appears on the branches but everything really came from the vine. Jesus is saying that if you want all the exciting grapes then you need to be connected to the vine. Makes sense right? If you chop a branch away from a tree it dies. It's just the same with a branch of a vine and it's just the same in our life with Jesus. We can't head out on our own and expect it to all be OK.

We must stay plugged in!

The gardener is God the Father

Jesus then brings God the Father into the picture. The Father is the gardener. The gardener looks after the whole plant. He makes sure there is enough water, the soil is of the right kind and He does something called pruning.

Pruning is where you cut off some of the plant. The gardener of a vine would do two types of pruning. He would cut off branches which haven't developed properly and which aren't producing grapes. This seems like a no-brainer to us. However, he would also cut off some of the new and healthy looking growth. This seems mad to us!

If you were listening to Jesus 2000 years ago you would

have understood the process that he was talking about. The gardener cuts off some of the healthy branches because then all the energy and nutrients of the plant is focused on just a couple of areas of growth so that these will produce lots and lots of fruit in the longer term. The plant can't see for itself which ones should be kept and which ones should be cut off. Only the gardener has the bigger perspective, the bigger picture to see what should be left and what should be cut off.

So what about the branches?

So you may be thinking 'this is all very nice but for those of us who don't want to be gardeners or winemakers what on earth is the point of all this?' Well, the point Jesus is making is all about connection.

Jesus is calling on us to be connected to Him whatever is going on in our life. We are the branches. That means that we can't always see the big picture of what God is doing. We are called to stay connected to Him whether we are being pruned by the gardener (God the Father) or whether we seem to be producing loads of fruit for God's kingdom. Our job is not to try and fight what God is doing but rather to stay connected to Jesus whatever God is doing.

To help us with staying connected to Jesus we use the **semi-circle tool**.

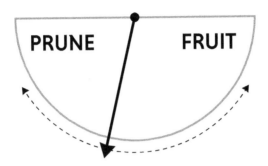

The semi-circle reminds us that God is always at work in our life in different ways and we are called to connect with Him whatever he is doing. Looking at the semi-circle I've drawn above, you can see that it works like the pendulum of a clock gently swinging between producing fruit and being pruned, with lots of space in the middle where both are happening at the same time.

This tool helps us work out what God is doing with us at any one time and how we can make sure we stay connected to Jesus whatever we are going through.

Producing fruit?

Sometimes we feel like we are in a time of producing fruit. Maybe everything feels like it's easy with God, the bible just seems to come alive, every prayer seems to change the world and people are coming to faith all around you. Maybe you're having real breakthrough in avoiding the sin that has been holding you back. Maybe you find that you are just having more patience than you've had before ... All of these are times when God is enabling us to be fruitful.

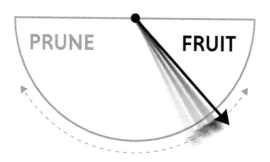

So if you're bearing fruit, what does your response need to be? You need to stay connected to Jesus. So don't be arrogant and proud and think that it's because you've cracked being a super Christian. In the fruit times of life remember to thank God for what He is doing in you. Spot where He is at work in your life and invest time in developing fully what He is doing. If you're seeing friends come to faith then make sure you spend plenty of time with non-Christians. If you are growing in patience then make sure you keep exercising that gift even when it's hard with your family. See what the Father is doing and get involved.

Being Pruned?

Sometimes, however, it doesn't feel like we are in a time of seeing fruit at all. Sometimes the bible doesn't seem to make any sense, our prayers seem to stop at the ceiling, our friends don't want to know about Jesus and it feels like patience is a million miles away! The good news when this is happening is that it's a very natural part of being connected to Jesus. God is allowing things to be pruned, cut back, removed. Jesus makes it clear that He's not doing this because we've done something wrong. Remember, the gardener cuts off some branches that are bad but he also cuts off things in our lives which are good because it will help to boost the really good stuff in the future. Our response is to take more time with Jesus, to thank Him that we know that He does things for our good and He'll lead us to a time of fruit in the future. Hang in there and invest in what you see God doing. If he is pruning something then make sure you allow it to be pruned.

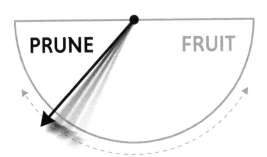

If God is pruning a bad branch, a sin or a pattern of behaviour which you know isn't helpful, then use the circle tool to engage with that learning moment.

If God is pruning a good branch, then get involved in what he is doing. Remember he is always wanting to help you grow in every situation, so take the opportunity to learn using the circle. How will you grow from this in the future?

The circle tool we've already learnt about in chapter 1 is helpful in both of these situations. The circle can help us process the learning moments which the semi-circle creates.

THINK ...

1. Are you in a time of fruit or a time of pruning?

2. What's your response to what God is doing?

Remember to use the Circle from chapter 1!

Other ways we see pruning and fruit

The semi-circle can also be used to help us see how God works in other rhythms in our lives. So, for example, you might like to see how God leads you to have different times of:

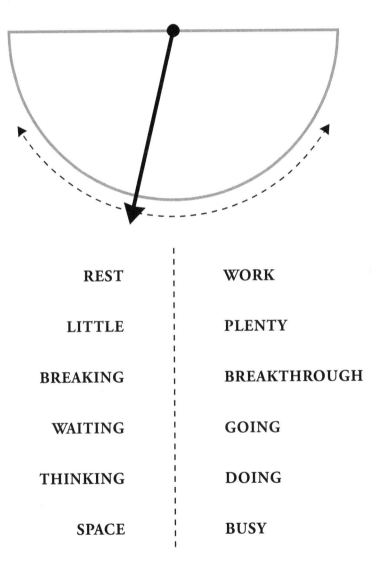

REST	WORK
LITTLE	PLENTY
BREAKING	BREAKTHROUGH
WAITING	GOING
THINKING	DOING
SPACE	BUSY

THINK ...

1. Is there one of these semi-circles that challenges me or speaks into my situation well right now?

2. What is God asking of me during this time to make sure I stay connected to Jesus?

3. How am I going to take this learning opportunity around the circle?

3

Have it all, all of the time

the Triangle

"**H**elp!!" I murmured as I crouched on the floor surrounded by hundreds of jeering teenagers and then that was it.

I had fainted.

I woke up to several hundred of the most entertained young people I have ever seen. I was 18 years old and I was on a gap year working for an organisation called Scripture Union in India. I had been helping out at a school, running activities and doing a little teaching. I had been excited to be invited to their end of year party as the oldest students were moving on. Some of the young people had organised a chilli eating competition as a bit of fun and I had been dared to enter. 'How hard can it be?' I thought, 'I like spicy food and these are just kids. I'm bound to wipe the floor with them.' The young people came up to me with chilli number 1 on a plate ready for me to eat. They had a bit of a glint in their eyes and were clearly looking forward to seeing the crazy English bloke get beaten by one of their own. We were ready for battle! I took chilli number one and munched it down with a triumphant look on my face. I was right. It was no problem. The last bite of the chilli was swallowed and I wondered just how many of these I could eat. Probably hundreds I thought and started to wonder about what the world record was.

And then the burning started.

Gently at first, as though I was being warmed by a radiator inside my throat, and then more and more and more until it felt as though someone had a flame thrower pointed down my neck. I started to feel dizzy, got to my knees as sweat poured down my face ... and then I fainted.

I literally never lived it down.

The most embarrassing part was that some little 13 year old kid won by eating 14 of them!

I learnt an important lesson on that day which helps us as we think about our next tool. Too much of a good thing can be a bad thing! You need balance in your life. You can't just have a diet of chilli. It does funny things to you!

God has made us to be people who live in balance. We need to have a varied diet, a varied life of different activities, and a varied life of different things to keep us entertained. Too much of one thing is either bad for us, boring or just simply means we're missing out.

We all know that God didn't just make us people of flesh and blood. He made us spiritual people. We have another element to our lives that needs to be lived out in a varied way. Our spiritual lives need to be in balance too.

There are three ways in which we live out this spiritual life which God has given us and He is calling us to invest in all of them in order that we have a healthy, mixed and interesting diet to feed this spiritual part of our natures.

The tool that we use to make sure we're living a balanced life is the triangle.

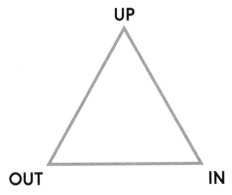

There are three corners of the triangle. Each corner represents one aspect of our walk with God.

UP

UP describes our connection with God. How close to God do we feel right now and how well do we think we are investing in our relationship with Him? In the Bible we discover that we are God's children.

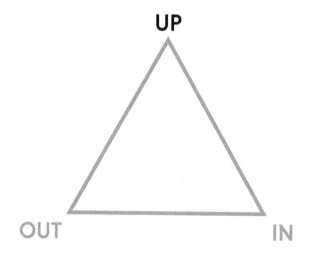

"See what great love the Father has lavished on us, that we should be called children of God! And that is what we are!"

1 John 3:1

Being children of God means we can have a relationship with

God ... Our Father. However, we need to put time and effort into making the relationship close. We wouldn't have a very good relationship with our dad, mum, brother, sister or friends if we never spent any time with them. We wouldn't even know what they are like!

To use this tool and see how our UP relationship with God is going we might think about how our prayer times are going right now, how well we are hearing what God is saying to us or how well we are doing at reading the Bible.

It's all of these things and so much more.

You may find it useful to use the questions at the end of this chapter (page 57), which we have developed from the 3DM huddle questions to help young people think through the different aspects of their walk with God.

You can download copies of this question sheet along with other resources to use with your youth group at www.timetorebuild.co.uk.

We can develop and grow in our relationship with God in so many ways and this UP part of the triangle is reminding us that it is vital that we invest in this important aspect of our Spiritual life.

THINK ...

1. If you were to score the UP aspect of your relationship with God out of 10 what would you give yourself? A 1 might mean you feel a million miles away from God right now and you can't remember the last time you read the bible. 10 on the other hand could be you feel like you are hearing His voice all the time and seeing Him in every situation with a scripture reference to boot. So what did you give yourself? Why?

2. Use the circle tool we looked at in chapter 1 to think about what you might do to improve or keep your UP score.

IN

IN describes our relationship with other Christians. The Bible shows us that if God is our Father then our fellow Christians are our brothers and sisters.

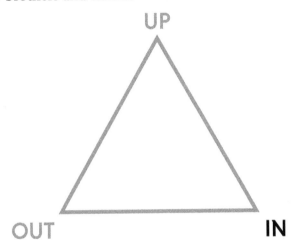

Finally, brothers and sisters, rejoice! Strive for full restoration, encourage one another, be of one mind, live in peace. And the God of love and peace will be with you.

1 Corinthians 13:11

This means that a key part of our spiritual walk is impacted by our relationships with our fellow Christians. A huge amount of the Bible is filled with the writers of the New Testament encouraging the early Christians to love one another. Just as we don't magically end up with a good UP relationship with God, we don't just show up to church and end up with a good

IN relationship with our Christian brothers and sisters.

To use this tool you will want to think about how good your relationships are with your friends, how much do you look forward to going to church or your youth group and how well do you feel like you're serving at church or your youth group. Again, it's this and so much more!

Have a look at the full questions sheet at the end of this chapter (page 58) to see all of the IN questions that will help you think through how your IN relationships are doing. Remember you can download copies of this resource at www.timetorebuild.co.uk.

In order for us to have a balanced walk with Jesus it's important that we invest in key relationships with our brothers and sisters in Jesus. We need to learn to love them, work well with them and serve each other so that we are all growing in our walk with God together.

THINK ...

1. If you were to score the IN aspect of your life out of 10 what would you give yourself? To give yourself a 1 might mean you feel like you hate your youth group right now and you can't remember the last time you went to church let alone

served anyone. A 10 would be you not being able to wait to get to church so that you can clean the toilets and give out free hugs for everyone on the way in. What would you score yourself? Why?

2. Use the circle tool we looked at in chapter 2 to think about what you might do to improve or keep your UP score.

OUT

OUT describes our relationships and engagement with people who are not yet Christians. We can be sure that this is important to Jesus because one of the last things He said to His disciples, after He had been raised from the dead but before He left earth for heaven, was about connecting with those who don't yet believe.

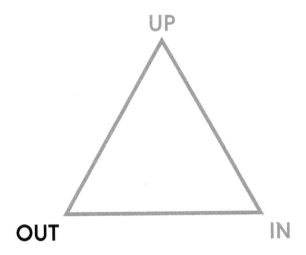

[8]Then Jesus came to them and said, "All authority in heaven and on earth has been given to me.[19] Therefore go and make disciples of all nations, baptizing them in the name of the Father and of the Son and of the Holy Spirit, [20] and teaching them to obey everything I have commanded you. And surely I am with you always, to the very end of the age."

Matthew 28:18-20

This is a very famous bit of the Bible that lots of us will have heard of before. However, we can miss that Jesus says something very challenging to his disciples. Jesus didn't say 'go and look after yourselves, hold onto the people you've got who already believe in me and try hard not to sin.' Looking after the people who already believe in God is important of course, we've just looked at the IN bit of the triangle. However, Jesus' last words to his most trusted leaders was to

*'go and make disciples **of all nations'.***

Remember, he is talking to people who are all from just one nation and yet Jesus' last command to them all is to look beyond themselves.

The truth that there is a God who loves everyone, wants relationship with everyone and has the gift of eternal life available for everyone, is really Good News. We need to share it!

The OUT bit of the triangle helps us think about how well we are doing at this key part of the Christian life.

To use this tool you may want to think about how much time you spend time with your non-Christian friends, how open you are about your faith in God, and whether you are looking for opportunities to lead people towards Jesus. Is your life bringing people towards God? It's this and so much more!

Again, have a look at the full questions sheet at the end of this chapter (page 59) to see all of the OUT questions that will help you think through how the OUT aspect of your walk with God is going.

In order that we have a balanced walk with Jesus it's important that we invest in key relationships with people who don't yet know Jesus.

THINK ...

1. If you were to score the OUT aspect of your life out of 10 what would you give yourself? If you gave yourself a 1 it might be that you have no non-Christian friends at all and you're terrified of even admitting that you believe in Jesus. To give yourself a 10 might be as if you have seen all of your school turn to Jesus and you're leading a church with your

headmaster. So what would it be for you? Why?

2. Use the circle tool we looked at in chapter 1 to think about what you might do to improve or keep your OUT score.

We're all different and as such we have lots of different strengths and weaknesses in life. This is true in our spiritual life as well as with everything else. Generally people are better at different bits of the triangle. For example, I am usually better at UP than I am at IN.

I often find myself getting frustrated with people in our church, usually really unfairly! I have had to work much harder at the IN part of the triangle than I have to work at the UP part. For you it may be a very different story.

THINK ...

1. Which part of the triangle are you usually best at?

2. Which part of the triangle are you usually worst at?

We all want to have a balanced diet. We need to have a balance to our lives which means working on all of the things we are less good at as well as keeping going with the things that come most naturally to us.

Youth Huddle Character Questions

Up Questions

Do I pray lots?

Do I feel close to Jesus?

Do I pray for things other than me?

Do I rely on God or myself?

Do I see God changing me?

Am I enjoying life?

Do I feel peaceful?

Am I afraid or nervous?

Do I do what God asks me to do?

In Questions

Do I love other Christians?

Do I use my time well?

Am I resting enough?

Are my friendships good?

Do I relate well to the opposite sex?

Do I keep my promises?

Do I trust people easily?

Do I disciple (invest in) others?

Are my relationships at home good?

Am I sleeping/eating well?

Am I being real with people?

Out Questions

Do I care that people don't know God?

Do I often share my faith?

Do I have non-Christian friends?

Am I ever tempted to give up?

Do I know what God is asking of me?

Do I try to get people to love me by being successful?

Am I proud of following Jesus?

Do I serve others?

Do I notice when people are interested in Jesus?

Can I take risks?

4

Following and leading well

the Square

"**H**ow long is it from here?" I asked, tentatively, trying to not sound as exhausted as I felt. I was walking with a big group of young people in the jungle in India. To be honest I was feeling pretty fed up. I had been asked by the camp leader of an outdoor pursuits activity centre to trek out on my own and meet up with a group, and then walk with them back to camp. I had dutifully walked out carefully following the directions I had been given, and met up with a big group of young people and a bunch of experienced looking leaders. We'd set off in the direction of the camp, but for some reason the walk back seemed to be a whole lot further than on the way out. I was therefore feeling pretty aggrieved with the guy who was in charge of the group who had been leading us back towards the camp.

To my astonishment rather than gently letting me know how long it was until we would be back at the camp he said,

'I've got no idea. Don't you know?'

'Oh no ... I didn't take this route on the way out to you' I said, through gritted teeth, whilst at the same time thinking 'what a plonker' to myself. I mean, fancy not knowing how long a trek takes before setting off and leading us all on this ridiculous path.

'I thought you would know where you were leading us,' he said to me with growing venom.

'WHAT?!!'

As it turned out he had thought he was following me and I had thought I was following him and somehow we'd aimlessly walked for hours without knowing where we were going. I'll leave you to imagine for yourself how well it went down with all the young people when we shared with them that we had gone miles in the wrong direction simply because we didn't know who was following and who was leading!

Leadership is such an important part of what God is calling each of us to as we think about the life we have ahead of us. Leaders influence things, change things and impact things and

Jesus calls us to all be world changers. This means every single one of us is called to leadership. I don't mean that we are all called to be church leaders. Leaders are simply people who lead people from one place to another. That means if you are helping one of your friends at school meet Jesus then you're a leader. If you're part of a campaign to make your street a more environmentally friendly place then you're a leader. If you're called to become a lawyer, teacher, builder, nurse or just about anything else, then you are a leader. We are all called to be leaders.

However ...

We're also all called to be followers. The best followers always make the best leaders. We all need to be leading well and we all need to be following well too. The Square is a tool that helps us think about leadership and following. Jesus had a bunch of followers in the Bible. These followers were called His disciples. These disciples (some of whom would have most likely been teenagers at the time they met Jesus) went from simply following Jesus around and trying to do what He did to being some of the most influential leaders who have ever walked the earth.

Not bad!

The square is all about following and leading well. We're going to track how Jesus led His disciples so that they became the incredible influential leaders that they were. Jesus was the best leader in the world but He was also the best follower. Jesus made it clear that even though He was the Son of God He still followed the direction of God the Father.

The square highlights for us four different stages of leadership which occur whether we're leading a prayer group, a multinational company or a church. Leading through these stages is what Jesus did with his disciples, and this helped them grow so well. The disciples were not, however, passive learners. They were active ones. We'll look at each stage of the Square and stop and think how we can follow well and how we can lead well.

Stage 1

The first stage of the square we call Disciple one (D1 for short) for the followers and Leader one (L1 for short) for the leader. This stage is usually a really exciting bit of the journey for everyone. It's where we

L1
Leader 1

D1
Disciple 1

set out on a new adventure together, take on a new challenge, join a new team or respond to a new vision. We can see this stage for Jesus and the disciples as Jesus calls them to be His followers at the beginning of their journey.

> *¹⁸As Jesus was walking beside the Sea of Galilee, he saw two brothers, Simon called Peter and his brother Andrew. They were casting a net into the lake, for they were fishermen. ¹⁹"Come, follow me," Jesus said, "and I will send you out to fish for people." ²⁰At once they left their nets and followed him.*
>
> *Matthew 4:18-20*

Jesus calls His disciples to an exciting new vision, a new task, a new activity. They had been fishing for fish but now Jesus calls them to follow him and he'll make them fishers of men. The reason they follow Him is because He gives them a big idea. A big plan. A big world changing vision.

The follower / disciple in D1

In D1 the role of the follower is to allow themselves to capture the big idea. They don't need to ask a million questions and stifle that idea with their own fears. A good follower hears the call to something new, something bigger, something which captivates them and they **respond**. There are so many people who hear a call to action from a leader, feel their hearts move with the vision and sit there and hope that someone else steps forward. If we want to be good followers then we have to be prepared to start the journey and say yes even before we really know what we're getting ourselves into. Do you think those first disciples really had any idea what Jesus was talking about when He called them to the vision of being fishers of men? I think they found a person they could follow, with a captivating vision that they were excited about and stepped out before they really knew all the ins and outs! D1 is about allowing ourselves to get excited and capture a vision!

The leader in L1

The role of the leader is to present a vision and invite other people into the journey with you. There are too many leaders out there who have a captivating vision of where they could go but are merrily getting on with going there all on their own. Jesus shows us a different way. He didn't even send the disciples out on their own to go and pick up a donkey! That's because Jesus believes in team. If you feel like you have something that you think God is calling you to do then your first question needs to be ... who am I taking on this journey with me?

What you have to realise as a leader is that your team at this point may well be unsure of what is going to happen. They'll probably be just as excited as you are and everyone will be blissfully unaware of any of the problems which may well happen on the journey. As a leader it's ok to go with it in this phase of leadership. Jesus didn't stop the disciples as they left their boats and say ...

'hold on chaps I'm not sure you've really understood me ... you see most of you will end up giving your lives for this.'

It would have been true but they wouldn't have been ready for it. They just wanted to get stuck into the exciting stuff. Allow the people who follow you to have the vision sink into their hearts in this L1 stage of leadership. Allow all the creativity to flow even though they probably won't have a clue what they're doing.

Stage 2

Stage two is called Disciple two (D2) for the followers and Leader two (L2) for the leaders. This is a tough part of the leadership journey. Inevitably in any project,

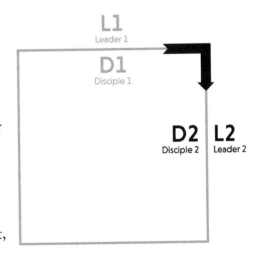

activity or vision the crushing reality of how hard the task ahead is going to be comes home to everyone. The blissful ignorance of D1 has passed and you're trying desperately to see something happen but it's proving to be a lot harder than you thought!

You can see this happen to the disciples that Jesus was leading.

> *¹⁷ Teacher, I brought you my son, who is possessed by a spirit that has robbed him of speech. ¹⁸ Whenever it seizes him, it throws him to the ground. He foams at the mouth, gnashes his teeth and becomes rigid. I asked your disciples to drive out the spirit, but they could not.*
>
> *Mark 9:17-18*

Can you imagine being the disciples in this situation? The vision Jesus gave them was that they would become fishers of men just like He was. They leapt headlong into copying everything that Jesus did, but then they started to realise that it was pretty hard. This was one of those times where they realised it was tough to be a fisher of men. They did everything Jesus told them to do and yet they couldn't heal the man. Jesus then steps up and with one word the son is healed! It must have been so frustrating. You can see that they wanted a nice simple solution from Jesus (later on in the passage) as to why they couldn't do it, but all Jesus says is that it would require prayer from them.

It's fitting that on the square, D2 is the arrow pointing downwards because this is exactly what it feels like for the followers (and to a great degree the leader) in D2 or L2. So how do we lead and follow well in this tricky time?

The follower / disciple in D2

The role of the follower or disciple in D2 is fairly simple. In short, DON'T GIVE UP! Can you imagine how tempting it must have been for Jesus' disciples to give up and go back to fishing after they made their thousandth mistake and been told off by Jesus for getting it wrong yet again? They must have started to doubt whether this 'fisher of men' thing was something they were really cut out for. It's easy as a disciple in D2 to try and pretend it's everyone else's fault. I'm impressed that the disciples' attitude to not being able to do what they felt they should, in the story in Mark 12, is to ask Jesus what they had got wrong. If I'm honest I think my temptation would have been to sling my hands in the air and whisper to my fellow disciple, 'well I thought the "healing of demon possessed people" was a very poor module on this discipleship course anyway. I'll give Jesus a terrible leader appraisal at the end of the year for teaching us so badly!'

It's so tempting when we realise that we're not very good at something to blame everyone else around us rather than face up to the fact that we're struggling ourselves.

The leader in L2

In L2 the leader has a tough role. There are two key things that the leader needs to do which we see in the way Jesus leads His disciples as they are struggling. The first thing we need to do is to remind everyone of why we started this journey in the first place. We need to remind the people who are following us what the destination is. You know when you're on a really long walk and you start to feel exhausted how important it is to remind each other what the prize is at the end (an ice cream, a cup of tea, an energy drink, etc). Well, it's just as important for the people that are following to be reminded of where they are going. The second thing that you will need to do for people following you in L2, is to give them lots of time and space to chat about what's going on, and lots of reassurance that you're all in it together. You'll notice when His disciples are struggling, Jesus starts to spend much more time addressing just His disciples and less time talking to the crowds.

Stage 3

The third stage of leadership is called ... you guessed it ... Disciple three (D3) for the follower and Leader three (L3) for the leaders. I know, we got seriously creative on this one!

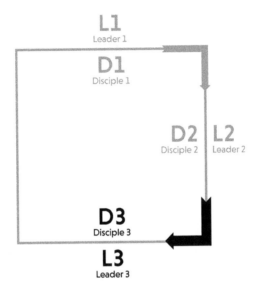

D3 and L3 are the part of the leadership journey where you start to see some breakthrough and steps start to be made towards the vision which we set out on in L1. Everyone starts to grow in confidence that the vision which was spoken about at the beginning of the process may actually be an achievable goal.

Again, you can see this in the disciples of Jesus when he sends out 72 of his followers to have a go at all of the things he was doing. We can capture a glimpse of their growing confidence in the report they bring back to Jesus about all that had happened after they had been sent out.

> *The seventy-two returned with joy and said, "Lord, even the demons submit to us in your name."*

> *Luke 10:17*

The disciple / follower in D3

The role of the follower at this point in the journey is to step out in the new confidence which they have discovered, without trying to run before they can walk! I always imagine it must have been tempting for the 72 disciples to return to Jesus and say ... 'Great, I think the training is done Jesus. Thanks for all you've done. It's time for me to take over the ministry now'. I mean it sounds crazy to us, but as breakthrough comes it's always tempting to think we've got it all nailed down.

The leader in D3

In D3 the leader's role is quite simple. It's time to allow your team more freedom to step out and try things. After making it through the tough time of D2 it's so tempting to try and hold onto everything but the leader has to allow the team to start flying. However, it's not time to leave yet. The team still need lots of feedback and advice so make sure you stick around and give it!

Stage 4

The final stage of leadership is called Disciple four (D4) for the followers and Leader four (L4) for the leader. This is where the team is really taking off, everything is going well and things have really developed. It's amazing when you're part of a team which has got to D4 because you actually see the vision begin to become reality. The challenge for the leader is that this is usually the time when God calls you to leave and pass the baton on to one of your team who is ready to step up and start their own process beginning at L1.

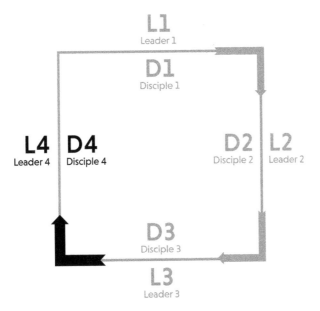

We see this with Jesus when He leaves His team just as they've all started to see breakthrough and He puts Peter in charge of the team.

> [8] *"But you will receive power when the Holy Spirit comes on you; and you will be my witnesses in Jerusalem, and in all Judea and Samaria, and to the ends of the earth."* [9] *After he said this, he was taken up before their very eyes, and a cloud hid him from their sight.*
>
> Acts 1:8-9

The follower / disciple in D4

As a disciple it's simple. It's time to step up and see how God is now calling you to lead. There's no point trying to cling on to what you had. The disciples tried to cling on to Jesus but He refused them and kept telling them that He had to go and that it was time for them to step up.

The leader in L4

The leader's job in L4 is to get out of the way and let the next generation of leaders loose. This can be really costly. Jesus had spent three years investing in His disciples, and then just when they started to get it right He had to leave them to it. He did this rather than getting to lead them at a time when it was easy and didn't really need Him anymore. Letting go at the right time is one of the most important lessons in leadership.

THINK ...

1. Can you think of a time when you've been at each of the different points on the square (D1, L1, D2, L2 etc)?

2. At which bits of the square do you find it easiest to be a follower or a leader?

3. Are you on the square in something right now? If so, where are you up to and how do you need to be following or leading?

5

How am I wired up?

the Pentagon

J ust recently I was doing some DIY in our house by putting a new plug socket in the wall. I went downstairs and turned off all the electricity for the upstairs of our house so that I would be safe while I worked. I started to take all of the bits of plastic off the wall and finally got to the bit when I could pull the old wires out. Whilst I was doing this my wife walked into the room and as I put my hand into the socket she walked over to me and punched me as hard as she could right in the face!

Or at least that is what it felt like!

As it turned out my wife hadn't punched me in the face at all, although it did take me several angry seconds to realise it. In fact, the person who had wired up our house had wired it up all wrong and so this socket, although being upstairs, was actually connected to all the downstairs electricity. As I had put my hand into the socket, 240v of England's finest electricity had flooded my body and it felt like someone had punched me as hard as they could in the face. Horrible, and I was lucky not to be hurt.

All too often we feel like we've been wired up wrongly in our walk with Jesus. So often I catch myself thinking ... If only I was more like them, they have all the cool spiritual gifts and seem to have it all together. The stuff they are really good at for Jesus is the stuff that Jesus prefers; I just need to be more like them!

The truth is that God has wired all of us up differently, uniquely and amazingly. Not one of us is wired up wrongly. However, Paul in the New Testament gives us a really helpful window to understand some of the differences we see in us Christians, which helps us learn about our strengths and weaknesses.

> *So Christ himself gave the apostles, the prophets, the evangelists, the pastors and teachers.*
>
> *Ephesians 4:11*

Paul here is listing the fundamentally different ways in which God has wired up his believers for different roles within the church.

Our next tool, the Pentagon, helps us think about these 5 different wirings that Paul shows us in Ephesians so that we can learn how to both invest in our strengths as well as grow in our areas of weakness.

As we go through these five different wirings think about which ones fit you best and which ones sound least like your strengths.

Apostle

The word apostle is a bit weird for us today. If you're like me, then when you first heard that some people are called to be apostles then you thought that they were some sort of special bloke in the Bible. There were apostles in the Bible

but there are also apostles today. The word apostle isn't used much in our everyday life today but it was a term that was well known to the people who first heard what Paul was saying. Apostle comes from a Greek word which means 'sent one'. So the question has to be: sent to do what? Apostles were people who were sent into a place to bring in a change in the culture. Just like before Mumford and Sons, the banjo wasn't seen as cool, before God's apostles go into a place, God and His ways aren't thought of as cool.

Apostles are people that are called to bring a shift to a group of people, to bring a shift towards the way in which God intended things to be. Apostles change the culture to be more like the way God intended it. All of us are, of course, called to do this to a certain extent, but certain people are wired up to do this more easily than others. For some people, changing the culture is second nature.

So how do you know if God has wired you up as an apostle?

Apostles usually find it easy to start things. Are you good at coming up with new ideas, getting people excited about them and making them happen? Maybe you've started new things at school, in your youth group or church. God wires up apostles with the natural ability to start new things. When this is used for God then He sends you into new situations to see new things started, in order that Gods way of doing things becomes normal there.

Prophet

There are lots of prophets in the Bible, but again we sometimes think that there aren't any prophets today. But there are! Prophets throughout the Bible are people who are good at hearing what God is saying and telling people about it.

In the Old Testament you'll have seen that the prophets spent most of their time telling off the nation and its leaders for getting it wrong. Thankfully, since Jesus came the role of a prophet has switched to sharing the things that God is saying to encourage, build up and equip people rather than just to tell them off! Of course, all of us are supposed to be listening to what God is saying, but people who God has wired up to be prophets generally find this comes easily to them.

So how do you know if God has wired you up as a prophet?

Prophets generally love lots of time to pray and listen to God, and this usually comes fairly easily to them. Maybe you find that as you chat to your friends at church you have a different sort of prayer life than they do. Of course they will all pray, but you may notice that you find it much easier to hear what God is saying both for yourself and for others.

Evangelist

We often don't get our ideas about who evangelists are from the Bible but from people who we've seen in our lives or heard about from recent history. When we think of evangelists we

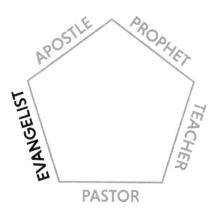

usually jump in our minds to the crazy looking people who stand on street corners shouting about Jesus or we think of shiny looking special Christians who appear on God TV or do big stadium events. These people may well be evangelists but they are the extremes. Evangelists come in lots of different shapes and sizes!

The main desire and strength of the evangelist is sharing about the Good News of Jesus with people who don't yet know Him. They are usually much more passionate about sharing the Good News with people that don't yet know Jesus than they are about helping people out who are already Christians.

So how do you know if God has wired you up as an evangelist?

Evangelists often come across a little like good sales people! Generally people want to do what they are excited about. If you're an evangelist then you'll probably find that friends will naturally become excited about the things that you're excited about. You may well be very aware of all the people around you in your friendship group, school or neighbourhood who don't know Jesus, and desire to see that situation change!

Pastor

PASTOR

I don't know about you but when I hear the word pastor I immediately think of a church leader. When Paul said that some people are wired up as pastors he wasn't talking about church leaders at all. He's talking about people who are brilliant at supporting people, loving them, and helping them grow into the person that God is calling them to be. They are like the shepherds of the church. Shepherds are famous for protecting their sheep no matter what comes at them and supporting them even if they get hurt. Pastors are fantastic with people that are struggling and finding life difficult, and therefore need support, help and challenge.

So how do you know if God has wired you up as a pastor?

Pastors are driven by their desire to help people grow and develop their faith in Jesus. You may find that your friends turn to you when things are difficult and they find it easy to share things with you. They may also tell you how much your advice and wisdom helps them. When they say these things to you it may surprise you, but it shouldn't because being a pastor is simply a gift God has given you.

Teacher

For most young people the idea of being a teacher isn't a very attractive one. We have an image of a Geography teacher with patches on their jacket droning on about the rules of the classroom. The Bible however gives us a very different picture! People who have the gift of being a teacher are those who are able to understand the Bible and bring others into that understanding.

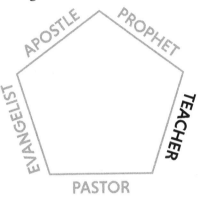

God has given them this gift to help keep the church on track with the core truths in the Bible and to make sure that we don't stray the wrong way in our thinking. They are the people who help bring us into greater understanding of what God has done for us and they use the Bible to help us understand more about what God is like.

What an exciting gift!

So how do you know if God has wired you up as a teacher?

Teachers are usually people who love reading the Bible and generally they hear what God is saying to them best that way.

85

Teachers usually bring correction to people by wanting to show them in the Bible where they have got things wrong. They are also people who usually get really excited by showing people new things they have discovered in the Bible. If you're a teacher your friends have probably mentioned to you that you seem to find reading the Bible easier than they do, although you may not realise that you are any different from anyone else … You may even get frustrated that others around you are less passionate about the Bible than you are. People may have also commented that they find things easy to understand when you describe it to them.

THINK …

1. Which of the 5 fold ministry descriptions do you most relate to and why?

2. Which of the 5 fold ministry descriptions do you least relate to and why?

3. Think about your friends and how they differ from you. Can you see which 5 fold gifts they might have?

6

Praying for all it's worth

the Hexagon

When I was first starting out as a youth worker, a group of my young people once called me over because they said they all wanted to pray with me. I was so excited! I had been trying to get them excited about prayer for ages and here they were asking me if we could all pray together. I tried to stay relaxed, not look over keen and keep my ice cool youth worker persona. I asked them how they wanted to pray and they said they wanted to all pray out loud together all at once really loudly and full of passion. I couldn't believe my ears. Obviously I had done such a good job of helping these young people grow that they were now flying with Jesus! My ice cool persona was lost and I couldn't help but tell them that I thought this was a brilliant idea. So one of the young people did a countdown and I launched in. I felt I needed to set a good example and encourage what was going on so I started praying at full volume, eyes shut in passion, hands waving in the air in a frenzy ... and then I realised something.

I was the only one praying. I petered out mid-sentence and opened my eyes to find out what was going on. As I opened my eyes the young people were videoing me and not one of them praying.

They fell about laughing.

It had been a trap and they had got me. Also, when I say fell about laughing I mean literally fell over and couldn't stop laughing for at least 20 minutes! It turned out to be one of those moments that took me a very long time to live down.

Our last tool is designed to help us learn how to pray. Praying is such an important part of our walk with God that even Jesus did it all the time. And yet, if you're like me, there may well be times when you don't find it easy.

Thankfully, Jesus' disciples were on the same journey as us and so they asked Jesus about prayer and He taught them a simple prayer full of truths and principles ... we often call it the Lord's prayer.

> [9] *This, then is how you should pray:*
> *Our Father in heaven,*
> *Hallowed be your name,*
> [10] *Your kingdom come,*
> *Your will be done*
> *On earth as it is in heaven.*
> [11] *Give us today our daily bread.*
> [12] *Forgive us our sins,*
> *As we also have forgiven people who have sinned against us.*
> [13] *And lead us not into temptation,*
> *But deliver us from evil.*
>
> *Matthew 6:9-13*

When we say this prayer we often say it just like this in church all together. There's nothing wrong with this, but Jesus meant it not only as something to be said as an exact copy but rather as a template for how to pray. So let's look at the contents of this template which Jesus gives us and think about how we should be praying.

God's Character

'Our Father in heaven,
Hallowed be your name.'

The first thing that Jesus
shows us to do is to focus
ourselves on who God is.
The start of this prayer is so
familiar to us that we can miss how amazing it is.

In the original language that Jesus spoke (it wasn't English
it was a language called Aramaic) the word which we have
translated as Father is the word Abba. Abba was the intimate
word that a child would use to address their Father. Daddy or
Dad would be the best equivalent for us to use today. Jesus is
telling us at the beginning of this prayer to address God not
as some impersonal distant God but rather as a close dad who
loves us.

He then goes on to say 'hallowed be your name'. The word
hallowed is a weird one, isn't it? I don't know about you but
I never use the word hallowed and to be honest I used to say
this prayer all the time and have no idea what I was saying
when I said those words.

The word hallowed simply means to *honour as holy*. Jesus is reminding us here that God is holy, big and powerful. He wants us to remember that when God spoke a word stars were flung into space. He's really very powerful and big.

The point that Jesus is making here is that when we come to God in prayer we need to remember that He is close. However, He doesn't want us to try and feel closer to God by bringing Him down to our level and making Him more like us. He wants us to be amazed, surprised and blown away every time we pray, that the God that flung stars into space ... that God ... is close and loves us.

That's a game changer for how we pray, and Jesus knew it!

He's powerful and He's close.

THINK ...

1. Are you better at thinking of God as your close Father or the mighty powerful creator of the universe? Which comes more naturally to you?

Do

1. Take a moment to pray to God and thank Him that he's both close and very powerful.

God's Kingdom

'Your kingdom come, Your will be done, on earth as it is in heaven.'

Then Jesus shows us that this powerful close God is a king and every king has a kingdom. Every king has a place where what they want to happen, happens. No questions asked. Here Jesus leads us to pray for God's

kingdom, God's way and God's will to be done on earth. Jesus is leading us to pray that the things that are going on in heaven break out on earth. Jesus not only prayed this prayer but He lived a life that expressed this prayer. This means we can see what it looks like when we pray this prayer. People choose to give rather than receive, people are drawn to God, sickness is healed ... the whole world is turned on its head! Heaven touches earth.

THINK ...

1. What do you think God's kingdom come would look like in your school, street, home or amongst your friends?

Do

1. Take a moment to pray for God to make your school, street, home or friends a little more like this picture today.

God's provision

'Give us today our daily bread.'

There's great news about this Father in heaven. The God that is close and yet powerful, the God that is King over a kingdom. The great news is that this amazing God is bothered about our basic needs. He is

bothered about the small things as well as the big things. He cares that we have enough food, shelter, clothing, health in our bodies and money so that we are sustained. Also, because He is the powerful God of the universe He has the power to do something about it if we need it!

Jesus teaches us that all we have to do is to ask God for our basic small needs. Jesus teaches us not to focus on the worries of the future but to rather consider what we need today ... now.

As we pray we are to simply ask God for what we need right now. This also shows us something of how often we are supposed to pray ... everyday. If we weren't supposed to pray every day then why would Jesus teach us to ask for our daily bread? If He had meant us to simply come to him every week then He would have taught us to say 'give us this week our weekly bread.' It's a daily thing. Bring Him your basic needs. Nothing is too small for Him to care about and nothing is too big for Him to be able to do.

THINK ...

1. What are your main needs today? What couldn't you do without?

Do ...

1. Take a moment to pray for God to give you everything you need.

God's Forgiveness

'Forgive us our sins, as we also have forgiven people who have sinned against us.'

Sin is a funny word isn't it. Often we think of preachers standing on street corners shouting at people and telling them that they are going to hell. This image has made the idea of sin a very unpopular one. The truth though, is that Jesus teaches us that all of us need to ask God for forgiveness. The reason is that all of us make mistakes.

God has set out a perfect way for us to live. Jesus showed us the way by living this perfect way and never sliding off the path that God has set out for all people. However, the rest of us find ourselves doing all sorts of things that God wouldn't have wanted for us. All of us need to ask God for forgiveness for not living out the perfect way which He has for us.

Jesus also shows us that we can't just accept the free forgiveness which God has given to us and not let it impact our lives. If God has given us this free gift then we need to make sure we pass it on. Often as we go through life people hurt us, wrong us, say bad things to us or treat us in a way we don't like. Just as God has been so generous in forgiving us, it's important that we also forgive all of the people that have hurt us. You don't need to wait for them to ask for it. You just need to take it to God and ask Him to help you.

THINK ...

1. Where and when have you not lived in the perfect way shown to us by Jesus this week?

2. Is there anyone you need to forgive in your heart who has wronged you?

Do ...

1. Take a moment to pray for God to forgive you and ask Him to help you as you forgive people who have hurt you.

God's Guidance

'And lead us not into temptation.'

Jesus knows that all of us have the potential to go the wrong way. The truth is there is an enemy (the Devil) that is trying really hard to convince us to go in a direction away from God. To do this the enemy tries to put temptation everywhere! Jesus teaches us to pray to God to lead us in a way that helps us avoid those temptations. In my experience God usually does this by prompting me to think twice before engaging in something that may well be a temptation for me.

When I was 16 I struggled with drinking too much alcohol with my friends. My friends would throw parties at their houses. I would go along and be determined not to drink too much. However, invariably, I would end up getting drawn into the fun at the party and get myself drunk. I started to feel a gentle unease in my heart about going to the parties and for ages I tried to ignore it. The truth was that this was God answering my prayer … 'lead us not into temptation.' Eventually I listened to this prompting from God and didn't go to any parties for 6 months. It was really tough but it enabled me to not drink too much. After that 6 months I had changed enough that I could occasionally go to the parties but I wouldn't be tempted to drink.

As we pray this part of the Lord's Prayer we need to make sure we are open to Him answering it. As He prompts us, often by a gentle feeling of unease in our heart, we need to make sure we listen. We asked Him not to lead us into temptation and He is answering us.

THINK ...

1. How might God be nudging you this week to help lead you away from temptation?

Do ...

1. Take a moment to pray for God to help you avoid that temptation.

God's Protection

'But deliver us from evil.'

The final part of the prayer
which Jesus teaches us to
pray asks God to protect
us as we walk through this
life. As I pointed out in
the previous section about
temptation we have an

enemy who is delighted when we mess up. The reason he is
delighted is because he wants to pull us away from God. The
good news is that Jesus is the one who has the power to keep
us safe from this enemy.

As we pray 'deliver us from evil' we are asking God to protect
us where we cannot protect ourselves. He is the mighty
powerful God who is also our Father that loves us. We can be
sure that when we pray and ask God to deliver us from evil He
will save us.

Jesus is our saviour both at the end of our lives but also right
here, right now. Jesus saves us every day.

THINK ...

1. Where do you need God to be your protector today? Where do you need him to save you?

2. Is there someone you know that needs Jesus to save them today?

Do ...

1. Take a moment to pray for God to be your saviour today. Pray also for those you thought of who also need God to be their saviour.

Conclusion

And finally, one last thing

I used to love playing a game on my computer called 'Worms'. In it you had lots of little worms which you would take into battle against another team. Each worm had a go at shooting at the other team until one team was victorious. When I first started playing the game I was terrible at it. The problem (I discovered later) was that I was only using the most basic gun which the worms had at their disposal. I hadn't realised that if I clicked a button in the top corner of the screen then I would have a whole tool belt of options available which enabled me to do all sorts of amazing things in taking on the enemy team!

LifeShapes are very like the tools at the disposal of a worms team … they are no use unless you use them! They aren't designed to be a course or book which you do one week and then forget about forever more.

You need to learn to use any tool well. I found this out on a building site I used to work on after hitting my thumb with a hammer a hundred times: I gradually learnt how not to hit my hand and how to hit the nails!

So, next time you have a possible learning moment I want you to think ... CIRCLE! Next time you're trying to lead something I want you to remember ... SQUARE!

Remember that in all you do God has so much He wants to bless you with. He wants you to learn and grow in every experience you have and so He will help you as you seek to use the LifeShape tools in your everyday life.

CPSIA information can be obtained
at www.ICGtesting.com
Printed in the USA
FFHW011015110120
57659568-63022FF

9 780990 777588